A JOURNEY TO NOW

A JOURNEY TO NOW

Success Strategies for Women & Minorities

LITA MARCELO ABELE

A Journey to Now

Publisher:
Lita Marcelo Abele

Publishing Consultant:
Professional Woman Publishing, LLC
www.pwnbooks.com

ISBN: 978-0-578-25256-8

Dedicated to those who wish to overcome the barriers to success,
and those who want to achieve their dreams

Acknowledgements

I owe my husband Merrill gratitude for giving me the opportunity to succeed and helping me fulfill my dreams. He has supported and encouraged me every step of my journey and in civic duties as well.

And my deepest gratitude to my children and family for their love and support.

To my second employer and family friend who helped and encouraged me to rise above.

Contents

Introduction

Success in life is not measured in dollars and cents. It is measured in the everyday things we do and how well we do them. In my growing up years I was not exposed to successful women. However, I did admire the actresses that played the parts of successful businesswomen. I dreamed that someday I would be one of them. I was not intimidated by being a woman in a man's world because of my strong determination to be a successful businesswoman. It's better to be respected than feared or loved. A mistake a woman entering the business world can make is expecting it to be easy....it is not. Work hard. Be persistent with a strong determination. Be honest with yourself and others.

Women and minorities face the biggest hurdles in the work arena. I know only too well, arriving from another country and being female, the challenges women face particularly in a male-dominated industry.

I will share my journey with you of how I started small, faced discrimination and in several instances abuse, only to continue with determination that these challenges were actually stepping stones to where my goals were set. Remember to never take your eye off the prize. Don't let anyone undermine your belief in yourself or your dreams....ever.

Follow me now as I share my humble beginnings, the move from the Philippines to the USA, and the tools used to land on my own two feet as CEO of a highly successful lumber company. If I can do it, so can you.

CHAPTER ONE

In the Beginning

Saying Goodbye

As I sat on the airplane, I was filled with both excitement and sadness. Leaving my family behind as I moved from the Philippines to the USA, was very painful. We had embraced and shed tears in the airport boarding area, and as I peered from my seat aboard the plane, I saw both my children with their little faces pressed against the glass looking, perhaps, for a glimpse of me in the aircraft window.

I was leaving everything and everyone I had ever known. I had been raised in a humble family with an abundance of love but not much money. There were many special and kind women in my life, but no successful businesswomen making a strong income to support their family. I wanted more for my children than my teaching salary could afford, and this was what fueled my determination to move to the USA, regardless of the fear.

My sweet little daughter loved Barbie dolls and wanted one so badly, but we could not afford this while living in the Philippines. I promised my daughter that when mommy had a new career and job that made good money, I would buy her a Barbie. And that was a promise I would later keep.

I had always had a mind of my own and was a very determined child from a young age. I had many dreams and visions of living a grand life someday, but in reality that had not come true during my early adult years. Yes, I excelled at school, was outspoken, intelligent, and challenged the norm, but there simply were no role models to guide me into a career where I could succeed in my home country.

With tears in my eyes, during my flight to New York City, I was filled with hope and anticipation that my new job in America, would provide an income and enough money, that I could send my beloved children to join me in the United States. Little did I know of the hell awaiting me in my new job position

Leaving my two small children in my home country of the Philippines was heart breaking but I stayed focused on my future in America and landing a new live-in nanny position for a family. This was going to be a dream come true!

After landing at Kennedy Airport in New York, I began working as a nanny but there were red warning flags already. I slept in a small cold room on a sofa and was not allowed to use the telephone or touch the refrigerator.

It was demanded of me to clean the house, cook all meals, babysit, while being treated with no respect and emotional abuse daily. This was hardly the American Dream I had envisioned. I was paid $150 per month and expected to work from 4:30am until midnight. I was cleaning and ironing clothes, cleaning the house from top to bottom (while being constantly criticized), being a nanny to the child, and being fed left-over food. I was basically treated like a slave.

When I could no longer stand the abuse, as a struggling mother who needed to work, I snuck to a pay phone and called upon a friend who introduced me to a married couple in need of a live-in baby sitter. I accepted the new position and made an escape from my abusive first employer.

My second employer treated me like family. I attended to the child with love and care and was made to feel so special. The employer moved after my hiring to Maine and took me with them where I worked for four years, again being provided with respect and encouragement to further my education, which I did with evening adult education courses. But the BIGGEST joy was about to take place. I was traveling with a friend to Boston, when I met the man I was to marry!

I was dining at an upscale restaurant and chatting with my friend when I noticed a handsome gentleman looking at me. He looked at me several times from where he was standing and finally I smiled at him. During the next hour, he introduced himself and joined us at our table. We exchanged telephone numbers and soon thereafter he invited me on tours of the city and dinner. He would travel from New Jersey to Maine to see me, and I traveled once to New Jersey. He began courting me within the following month with daily phone calls and flowers. And several months later he asked my father in the Philippines for my hand in marriage. My father granted permission and I happily accepted. My dream was coming true!

Once married, I moved to New Jersey with my husband and began taking classes at Glousester County College with the intention of becoming a nurse. I always wanted to be a nurse but science and I didn't get along! (I had taken previous adult education courses in accounting, computers, and other business-related subjects, which would eventually provide me with a strong foundation of knowledge to run US Lumber). My husband also said that since I had worked and supported myself for many years, it was time to step away from becoming a nurse, and instead I began to learn the ropes at my husband's lumber company. He had always wanted his wife to work with him. I had no idea that someday I would be able to send my children to America and that they now would help to run the lumber company which is over 5-10 million dollar minority owned business. Dreams come true and in very large part due to my husband believing in me and providing such strong encouragement.

But starting work at my husband's lumber company at a low-level position had its challenges! Fellow co-workers did not like me and made it very clear that they resented working with the wife of the CEO. I answered phone calls, sat in a small cubicle, worked with clients and vendors, and started learning more about the lumber industry daily. No matter how hard I tried to be part of the team, the employees did not accept me. This did not deter me from doing my job and doing it well! I learned many skills of rising above challenges by this beginning position in my husband's lumber company. I've never been ashamed of anything and working at a low -level position within the company provided the perfect environment for learning the tools needed to be a success in the lumber industry. I was teased about my accent and overlooked as a professional woman by clients and vendors.

My husband and I decided it best for me to start a lumber brokerage company, US Lumber & Plywood, more than two years later, it was decided my husband would semi-retire and that we would merge my brokerage firm with his company Silver Lake Lumber, and I became the CEO, while bringing my expertise and clients to the merged company.

Imagine a minority woman who was once a Catholic school teacher and housekeeper, running a company in the male-dominated lumber industry! My dream since I was in the Philippines was to be a boss. If you're hardworking with determination, perseverance and common sense, chances are you are going to be quite successful!

It was in 1993 that I grabbed the reigns and have been president and CEO of U.S. Lumber ever since. I'm very fortunate that I met my husband as he's the one who really gave me the opportunity to be where I am now. I read every article on lumber and was basically self-taught about expanding US Lumber to a new level of success. I learned the business from the ground up. I'm a dreamer and I dreamed that someday I could have my own business and when my husband gave me that opportunity, I took it. However, it was not without challenges as many employees did not to work for me as CEO, and several quit.

My husband and I became the sales team and after he fully retired, I was the only one in charge of sales.

I have worked long hours since the beginning in the U.S. Lumber office and enjoy every minute of it. One of my highlights with clients, is that most remember me as a highly professional woman with an accent! Oftentimes I have heard from clients and vendors that they cannot understand me. I learned English as a second language in the Philippines and take great pride in my accent and really do not work at losing the accent which helps to distinguish who I am when calling a client or vendor. Many clients consider me to be a powerful minority woman, not realizing I am 4'11" tall! I can stand with confidence in this male-dominated lumber industry regardless of stature or accent!

Single-handedly, I have kept the books, written the sales letters, made cold calls, trained the staff, and clearly never slept much. I visit job sites, attend professional meetings, and manage the company's niche specialty which is selling plywood products to concrete contractors to use as building forms for concrete used in bridges, highways, sports stadiums, and the list goes on and on. Yes, there's fierce competition, but we counter it with a service cocktail of fast 24-hour order turnarounds, a warehouse that can accommodate the commodities I buy by the carload and the ultimate in courtesy. Lots of pleases and thank-yous, and I'm the first to testify, it all boils down to rapport.

Most people might say I have climbed to the top and made it. I'm CEO of a successful lumber company, married the love of my life, my adult children work for the company, I am self-taught, and I'm the same person I was before my professional success. I'm happy I can afford to buy clothes, to out to eat dinner and buy a car, but money is not everything for me. It is not number one! I feel I still have to work hard and help people.

As I became more successful, I have contributed to small scholarships for impoverished Philippine students to buy books and food or whatever is needed, attend college at Rowan University by creating an exchange program with the University of the Philippines. I have been in their shoes when you want something but don't have the money. I can create the opportunities I didn't have, and if they become successful, that's also my success.

CHAPTER TWO

Breaking Diversity Barriers with Strength and Structure

"If we are to achieve a richer culture, rich in contrasting values, we must recognize the whole gamut of human potentialities, and so weave a less arbitrary social fabric, one in which each diverse human gift will find a fitting place."

— Margaret Mead—

Starting a new life can be full of joy and possibilities. Depending on from where and from whom you've come, it might also be fearsome and full of challenges. In fact, emigrating from another country with the intent to start a new life can be the loneliest place on earth, no matter where you are. What does that mean for those attempting to break through the barriers? It means that we've had to work harder and smarter than people without diversity challenges – cultural, racial or otherwise.

What does being "different" actually mean anyway? Wikipedia says that 'diversity' is the description of a group by which its members have identifiable differences in their backgrounds or lifestyles [1]. We live in a world where diversity is widely accepted, even expected. In fact, more than 38.5% of people residing in the United States come from other parts of the world and are considered foreign-born by the United States Census Bureau [2]. So why do minorities still find the barriers of style, culture and language to be so challenging, yet others are able to break through these common barriers and go onward to exceptional personal and professional success? I can only tell you my story with the hope that you will learn, as I have, to be a better builder of the structures that support your life.

Finding Your Strength

1 **Be a "Big Picture" thinker** – For most immigrants, we come to this country with hopes for the American Dream and the promises of opportunity for a better life. The key is to remember, in the face of adversity, who you were when you gave birth to these dreams. Don't lose sight of the idea that something better lies ahead, no matter how difficult the struggle may be to get there. Embrace unexpected opportunities, of which there will always be, and maintain a vision of optimism on the big prize (whatever that is to you).

2 **Observe using eyes & ears** – We have the ability to observe in silence when people aren't expecting us to be fully responsive. This can be an amazing asset for learning. Observation is one of the most powerful of human skills, for with it we learn to adapt and adjust to our changing environments.

3 **Ask for help. Don't keep secrets.** Adversity can only tear down your structural resolve if you choose to live with it silently. There is no shame in asking for assistance, with problems or big ideas,

but no one can help if you remain dishonest about your needs. In fact, most people actually seek ways to help each other for the simple human fact that it feels good to make others feel good. Take advantage of the ability to join forces, create partnerships, seek mentors and use good advice.

Taking Personal Assessment

1 **Never hide your talents** – One of the greatest gifts we have is that of being different. That means we have a variety of experiences and knowledge that no other individual has. In coming to America, I promised myself that I would never hide my talent and abilities, for that would allow another person to feel more powerful than me. In fact, this idea is central to my personal philosophy as I am now better able to celebrate and harness the true talents of others. Why would one individual silence their superior voice, when *everyone* stands to benefit from its wisdom?

2 **Self-teaching** – You may never lose the accent with which you've learned to speak English, but there will never be a reason not to READ, READ, READ. Read anything you can get your hands on and let yourself be saturated with new ideas, thoughts and information. While it is commonly said that 'knowledge is power', nothing could be more true in the life of an immigrant or a foreign-born minority. Remember, the voice in your head doesn't have to speak perfect English.

3 **Structured-teaching** – Additionally, seek out opportunities to learn from others in your desired field of expertise. Go to seminars, attend conferences, use the internet, join chat rooms and take online classes. Much of the information available on the internet is completely free and accessible at libraries, universities or community centers. Always keep in mind that adult education is worthy and necessary, but most of your applied knowledge will come from

your life's experience. Be proud of having a different history to teach to others and above all, embrace yourself first.

Strategies for Leadership & Business Building

1 **Increasing Visibility –**

a **Networking strategies –** Getting into the public eye and increasing your promotion efforts starts with networking. For minorities, a large part of this involves the bravery to immerse yourself with others; it takes the guts you have gathered by finding your strengths and taking self-assessments as discussed above. Accomplished those components and join local organizations that can expose you to new people, new opportunities and the tools to increase business. Joining your state and local Chamber of Commerce is a must. Networking groups such as BNI (Business Networking International at *www.bni.com*) have local chapters in every city. Additionally, seek organizations that feature regularly scheduled networking events with like-minded individuals, such as the National Association of Women-Business Owners at *www.nawbo.org*. More information on Minority and Women's Organizations are discussed below.

b **Building your business backbone –** Learn about ways your company can promote and implement cultural diversity resources at work. Subscribe to an informative newsletter at *http://www.diversityhotwire.com/subscription.html.*

2 **Finding Support –** There are many resources available to minorities. First and foremost, building a good relationship with your **local bank** is a strategy that lays the foundation for your future and business endeavors. Communication with your bank starts

with being honest about your goals, your business plans and your current limitations. Remember, it never hurts to ask. Once you become a trustworthy and dependable client, your requests will be answered more and more favorably.

- **Small Business Administration** – There is an SBA office in almost every city and is intended to be a resource for any business, minority or otherwise. Your state government websites will lead you to the nearest location in your area, as will the federal government's website at *www.sba.gov*. There you will find information about learning annex's in your town, business trainings, certifications and counselors that are willing and able to help you build business plans, grant requests, loan applications, etc. Many of these services are free of charge and are worth the time to research.
- **Minority Organizations** – Various organizations exist for providing ongoing support and certifications to women and minorities. Most certifications are granted for Minority or Women owned businesses, Small Disadvantaged Businesses, and Under-utilized businesses[3] in order to provide better business opportunities and can be found at *www.mwbe.com*. Here you can search for reading material, resources, group information and upcoming events as well as a full list of assisting public agencies. The U.S. Department of Commerce hosts the Minority Business Development Agency at *www.mdba.gov* and also features an array of business tools and opportunities.
- **Women's Organizations** – Both the National Council for Women's Organizations (*www.womensorganizations.org*) and the National Organization for Women (*www.NOW.org*) are great starting points for seeking both national and local organizations that assist and support women and minorities in

their efforts to increase learning, business and marketing opportunities. A strategic way to become involved in your own local area is to search online for organizations that specifically involve your culture, race or religion. For instance, as an Asian-American, I have made strides to become involved with several groups, including my local Asian-American Chamber of Commerce and the National Association of Professional Asian-American Women. A quick online Google search will uncover opportunities of your own.

3 What to AVOID

- Avoid envious people. Inevitably they will twist your intention and inhibit your growth out of sheer jealousy. This is no reflection on you, but rather an indication that they are unsatisfied with their own results. They'd rather not admit to themselves that while you are the one facing the challenges of looking or speaking differently, they themselves have no excuse.
- Avoid gossip and avoid talking down to others. Ignorance has no 'first language'. Putting others down or behaving as if you know more than they do make a negative person of you. Open-mindedness is the key to having effective communications, without which we cannot succeed in understanding each other, language barriers or not.
- Avoid hiding that you are different. If you behave as if being different is anything but exciting and new, people will follow suit with your example. Be proud of your differences and teach them something about you and your culture whenever you have the chance. This sharing of backgrounds only makes everyone stronger and smarter.

Addressing Negativity

"I do not want my house to be walled in on all sides and my windows to be stifled. I want all the cultures of all lands to be blown about my house as freely as possible. But I refuse to be blown off my feet by any."

— Mohandas K. Gandhi —

For every kind and helpful person, there will be one or more negative people that react to your diversity with rudeness or impatience. Those negative people let diverse backgrounds or language barriers get in the way of getting to know who you are and what you can offer. Let's face it, those people are missing the opportunity to benefit from you – and that's their problem, not yours. Nevertheless, you need to know how to encounter them so that their negativity does not limit your own progress or self-esteem.

Tips & Tactics

- No room for shame. Do what you must to regularly remind yourself that you've already come a long way. You see your future and you are aiming high for it. Despite the hard road ahead of you, you have made the decision to improve yourself and your life… and there is absolutely no shame in that.
- Use your sense of humor. An excellent way to disarm a negative person is to laugh it off or poke fun of the situation before they have a chance to do it. This does NOT mean embarrassing yourself or acting shameful. It simply means taking away their option to poke fun of you by creating an environment of acceptance and compassion about your challenge. For example; if you can tell by the look on someone's face that you may have used the wrong

word, lightheartedly laugh and say, "Oops…what did I just say? I think I meant to say__! What do you think?"

- Use your accent as a memorable marketing tactic. After over 20 years, my accent is still the best part of me – my friends and clients never question who is calling on the phone! Consequently, this also differentiates me with my business prospects, and I don't hesitate to point it out at each opportunity. They'll never forget who I am because of the accent; it's up to me to give them a favorable impression of the rest of me.
- Shake hands like you mean it. Be proud of who you are and extend that hand with confidence at networking events and/or business meetings. Always wear a nametag that identifies you immediately so that in the event that someone does not understand the pronunciation of your name, they can read it while they hear you say it. Be prepared to repeat yourself but don't take it personally. In most cases your patience will be noticed and appreciated.

Conclusion

Always remember that someday you will be better than the people who mistreat you today. You can feel shame and you can feel frustration, but you can also remain strong at the same time. In fact, it is while you experience these challenging feelings that you must be stronger than ever before, look adversity in the face and say, "Someday, you will know who I am."

Bibliography

1 *www.wikipedia.org/wiki/diversity*

2 2008 Factfinder at *www.census.gov*

3 *http://www.mwbe.com/cert/certification.htm*

Additional Resources

www.raceandhealth.hhs.gov
www.targetmarketnews.com
www.catalystwomen.org

CHAPTER THREE

Goals for Successful CEOs

Necessary Skills for CEOs

Fundamentally, a CEO must possess skills that embrace a clear corporate vision while maintaining flexibility in how he or she approaches challenges that threaten the corporation's financial viability.

When I served as an expert commentator for south Jersey's largest newspaper and offered commentary on the 2004 episodes of *The Apprentice*, I looked for an individual among the prospective candidates who had CEO potential. The qualities I sought among those interviewed were superstar tendencies, strong teamwork qualities, attention to detail, and an ability to be innovative under pressure to get the job done.

In strategic hiring among larger corporations, I am sure that when young, talented people are recruited, there is attention paid to whether they have the ability to rise in the company and contribute in strategic ways.

In my family-owned lumber company, I am the largest stockholder, with my husband owning the minority share. My children also work at the company, and I have 12 outstanding employees who helped our company earn over $6 million in sales in 2005. At this time, I am not hiring senior management professionals, but if I were, I would employ a talented person who understands finances, and who could help negotiate strategic partnerships among larger corporations seeking to retain women and minority-owned firms as consultant partners. I would want a professional who embodies many of the outstanding qualities of individuals who applied to be Donald Trump's apprentice.

My clients have my cell phone number, and often will find that I have surprise visits to their construction sites or offices where I can receive an instant assessment of how well my company is doing in quality control and the delivery of outstanding services.

Appropriate Times to Change an Organization's Vision

Usually, my leadership vision will change in moments of crisis, and in particular, if profitability falls. The changing global marketplace has required my business to implement outstanding business practices for superb customer service practices. Sometimes, even when my company is operating at peak performance, there will be changes in procurement or CEO vision at one of my client's firms that may still result in my losing this business. But I know that the decision had little or nothing to do with the manner in which U.S. Lumber conducted professional relationships with clients. Sometimes, it just has to do with other strategic considerations beyond my control. In the case where I may lose a client, I communicate to my employees what happened and how it was beyond all of our control.

The Effect of Globalization

With the emerging global market in all private-sector industries and services, my business must be a lean operation, with no or little waste, and outstanding customer service. I recognize that my clients also are under the same constraints and seek to maximize their profitability, as do I. Part of my CEO strategy involves being a hands-on customer service representative for U.S. Lumber, Inc.

Best Piece of Advice Frequently Given to Employees

The best advice I give my employees is, "Work hard, and you will be rewarded." As a hands-on CEO, I am in the business every day, and see operations and my employees. I employ men and women who are polite, hard-working, and take pride in their jobs. Many are immigrants or former immigrants like me, and they have been personally touched by the American dream when they came to America. To show my appreciation, I will cook lunch for them, bring them watermelon and other fruits on days of excessive heat, and I cover all their medical expenses through the payment of the health insurance premium and no co-payment.

Best Advice Received From Another CEO

The best advice I received from another CEO was to be open-minded and creative. I apply this advice daily, because I try to empathize with those who communicate their viewpoints about U.S. Lumber, my team, and business in general. Communication can only occur when we are listening to each other. Therefore, being opened-minded is key to engaging in a dialogue.

Resources for Staying Current with Industry Trends

Being active in the following organizations enables me to be on top of trends for my industry, the work of minority- and women-certified firms, and organizations that advocate on behalf of Asian-Americans: American Subcontractor Association; Greater Philadelphia Chamber of Commerce; National Association of Women Business Owners; National Association of Women in Construction; National Minority Supplier Development Council of PA, NJ, and DE; National Pan-Asian American Chamber of Commerce; National Women Business Enterprise; New Jersey Asian-American Chamber of Commerce; New Jersey Association of Women Business Owners; and Chamber of Commerce of South Jersey. As CEO, I must decide where our company's visibility is most effective for strategic partnerships and opportunity for business growth.

Establishing and Maintaining Brand Identity

CEOs of small corporations are often viewed as the firm's brand identity. I am the voice of U.S. Lumber. When I am interviewed for *Enterprising Women Magazine*, *Asian Enterprise Magazine*, *Philadelphia Business Journal*, *NJBIZ*, *Courier Post*, regional daily and weekly newspapers, people listen to my advice because I am a nationally recognized entrepreneurial leader. In business, we cannot afford to make unnecessary adversaries, and I work very hard to maintain a professional advocacy role for my company, in addition to leading on behalf of women- and minority-owned companies.

Three Golden Rules for a Successful CEO

My three golden rules for successful CEO leadership are:

- Never lie.
- Always remember that you are in business to please your customer.
- Be professional, courteous, and kind.

My advice to would-be CEOs is to always tell the truth, because once your credibility is compromised, there is no return to grace. I am proud to say that my word stands true. We must also remember that without our customers, our businesses would close. Therefore, be considerate of your customers and work with them to implement a vision that allows your business to thrive while providing excellent service. I cannot emphasize how important it is for CEOs to maintain a professional demeanor while being courteous and kind. I do not like mean people, and do not surround myself with anyone who is rude. As I have said in my speeches to business and community audiences, treat people with the respect levels that you demand from yourself and others. Kindness goes a long way, especially when it is genuine.

Three Tips for Success in Life

I also offer 3 tips for success in life:

- Embrace who you are and accept your unique assets.
- Never hide your talent.
- Always be thankful for those who helped you.

Embrace Who You Are and Accept Your Unique Assets

Let me highlight tip one for success in life. Some people automatically dismiss individuals with accents. For example, New Jersey is such a melting pot, a true land of opportunity, which has been the new entry for many immigrants. Many of us had family who arrived in America through the Port of New York, and our parents, grandparents or great-grandparents had accents. Unless people were brought here as slaves, most of our families came for the promise of opportunity, to make a better life, to seek freedom.

That's why I came, leaving behind my life in the Philippines. I still have my accent, which is an important part of me. My accent is my best public relations tool because no one forgets me after we meet. I embraced my accent and it helps me grow my business daily.

Never Hide Your Talent

I began my new life in America as a domestic worker, and was held against my will by my first American employer. I remember those times with sadness, and then I remember that I triumphed. One day, I had the courage to call for help. I called the very agency my employer threatened to call to have me deported. I called in the Immigration

Naturalization Service, the INS. That call helped save my life and my soul. It takes great courage to stand up against a tyrant, and from the moment I began my "new" life in America, I promised that I would never hide my talent and abilities to allow another person to feel powerful. This idea is central to my personal philosophy, and a good CEO knows that by harnessing the true talents of others, the company wins.

When I received numerous national honors from 2004 to 2006, an amazing opportunity opened for me. My recognition gives me an opportunity to speak and showcase my life experience as an immigrant, an Asian-American, and a woman who owns a non-traditional business. Why would I silence my voice? People listened as I discussed the need for more corporations to embrace diversity and share resources and power with those of us who have other cultural experiences. Be proud of your background and your unique attributes, and through your leadership others will follow. When each of us speaks freely, we educate others about our experiences, and open the door for growth opportunities.

Always Be Thankful for Those Who Helped You

As an immigrant who came to America and then was held, against my will and threatened with deportation, my story may be a little different, but gratitude and thankfulness is still the same.

For me, America has provided me with many experiences, and from the good and the bad, I have constructed some life lessons on how wonderful my life has become through a vision of optimism, experiencing unexpected opportunities, and finding love. It is still my faith in the goodness of people and the power of love that moves me, and I hope moves others.

When one gives from the heart, in my case, time, advice, and resources, the honor of recognition is never considered. Coming from the Philippines, I knew arriving in America would change my life forever. But my life is so different from what I expected and becoming a CEO of a successful company was one of the unexpected byproducts.

CHAPTER FOUR

Building and Maintaining a Strong Company Culture

The Crucial Role of a Robust Corporate Culture

Unless each business has a strong company culture that rewards leadership and outstanding services, the organization will languish. Yes, mediocre companies can yield profitable results; however, I believe that the profitability is a short-term gain because poor management practices and the absence of company loyalty will indeed undermine a company's foundation.

Keys to Developing Positive Culture

Because U.S. Lumber is still a small business, there is a greater flexibility in how we can set the tone for corporate culture and address management practices. We have much less of a hierarchal structure that inhibits creativity and innovation. My door is always open for employees to make suggestions about improving work operations or management practices, and I believe that the key to innovation is an openness to hear alternative viewpoints!

Open-Door Policy and Hands-On Leadership

Thankfully, I am actively engaged as a hands-on CEO, who works daily in the company office. In fact, my office is about 40 feet from the door leading to the warehouse and plant operations. Our company wants everyone, from the CEO down to floor workers, to be the best they can be and provide outstanding services. Excellence in customer service and product delivery are among the hallmarks for our women- and minority-owned firm.

With only 12 employees, my role incorporates serving as CEO, President, leading salesperson, and I assume the duties of an HR professional. We have worked with a communications/public relations consultant, but we tend to limit our dependence on independent contractors.

Typical Clients

To help understand how the company's corporate culture emphasizes excellence, I must first describe U.S. Lumber's corporate clients past and present. U.S. Lumber is a leading lumber supplier throughout New Jersey, Delaware, Maryland, and Pennsylvania. U.S. Lumber's past and present clients include DuPont Company, Philadelphia Gas Works, Exelon Peco Energy, Merck & Company, Madison Construction , Carson Concrete, Mumford & Miller, Healy Long & Jevin, Quinn Construction,Weatherby Construction and most recently, Atlantic City's relatively new Borgata Casino. When Philadelphia Eagles & Philadelphia Phillies fans walk into the team's two stadiums, U.S. Lumber's plywood is throughout the stadium, and her company was part of the Septa Transit Project built by PKF Mark III. For several years, U.S. Lumber will continue to supply lumber and plywood for the Driscoll Bridge repairs funded by the New Jersey Highway Authority.

The Trenton Route 29 Tunnel, the US Postal Service Project, and construction at Temple University constructed by B. Peitrini and Son all include U.S. Lumber materials. The New Jersey School Construction Corporation (NJSCC) contracted with an approved construction company that retained U.S. Lumber as one of the project suppliers.

U.S. Lumber carries a full line of building materials and products, including:

- Lumber, plywood, and allied supplies
- Treated materials
- Metal studs and track
- Insulation
- Moulding
- Sheet rock, spackle and tape
- Nails
- Plastic laminates
- Pre-finished and natural plywood
- Hardwoods — rough and surfaced
- Trusses
- Softwood and dimension lumber
- Mixed hardwood
- Crane mats
- HD plywood

A Role Model for Women- and Minority-Owned Businesses

Because we receive contracts from high-profile firms for extensive construction projects, U.S. Lumber is positioned to be a viewed as a representative example for all women- and minority-owned contractors.

Therefore, I take this advocacy responsibility quite seriously, and create a corporate environment that rewards excellent services with company bonuses annually in years where we have growth and where health care costs do not grow significantly.

Rewarding Excellent Customer Service

My employees know that I put myself on the line daily as the lead salesperson for our outstanding wood products. Therefore, I would argue that our corporate culture emphasizes outstanding services and customer service. In many ways, I communicate to my warehouse employees that they are engaged daily in providing the "best customer service" to me, their employer, and I reward those who advocate for the company by working hard to deliver superior work practices. Great customer service builds outstanding client loyalty to our company.

Business Week featured in its August 3, 2006 edition a feature article that noted that when it comes to customer loyalty, trust is the key to building and maintaining your customer base. This means working to build trust not only in the company, but also in the products, sales reps, marketing strategies and the industry. The *Business Week* article highlighted five trends that every successful business much accomplish with customer relations, and I am proud to say that U.S. Lumber excels in each:

- Build trust in your company.
- Build trust in your products and services.
- Build trust in you.
- Build trust in your marketing.
- Build trust in your industry.

Responsibility and Process for Refining the Corporate Culture

In meetings with my warehousing employees and my front office staff, I explain that when I can open doors to more business, the entire company will share in the beneficial results. Every activity I undertake is tied to supporting business growth and reinforcing our company image. Therefore, I would argue that all my time as CEO and the company's lead salesperson reinforces the building and maintaining a strong company image that is achieved through a realistic and understood company culture. In fact, I anticipate dedicating a portion of my time this November to evaluating company growth trends in order to determine if we need to adjust any policies and implement new ideas to enhance the company's profitability and expansion. Nonetheless, it is my responsibility to be the chief innovator for U.S. Lumber, and I would say that because I hear the views of all my employees and am active outside of the company, I am probably responsible for 75 percent of the influence in how the corporate culture is reinforced and improved upon.

Corporate Advocacy

As the lead salesperson for the company, U.S. Lumber invests in me when I participate in national advocacy and professional membership organizations past and present such as the National Association of Women Business Owners, the Chamber of Commerce of South Jersey, the National Association of Women in Construction, National Minority Supplier Development Council of PA, NJ and DE, and National Pan-Asian American Chamber of Commerce. By being visible, U.S. Lumber is viewed as a credible representative of women- and minority-owned companies. When my company or I are honored by various national, regional, and statewide business and community advocacy organizations, U.S. Lumber is recognized as a successful innovator and business leader, and that helps our relationships with suppliers, vendors, and clients.

Cultivating an Innovative and Diverse Workforce

The Role of Background

Innovation is in the eye of the beholder. This is a point I often make, because what appears to be innovative to one leader may be much less so to another.

In my family-owned lumber company, I am a Filipino immigrant who is now an American citizen. My company is certified as a minority- and women-owned business, and I represent a small but growing portion of the industry that has been traditionally dominated by Caucasian men.

So, it is important to recognize that when a woman with my background turns up as the CEO and President of an American lumber company, some heads will turn. My charge is to demonstrate to the traditional lumber leaders, senior management, and owners that U.S. Lumber, Inc. can do the job and perform it with the utmost professionalism and distinction.

Recognizing the Importance of Minority Growth in the US

The US Census Bureau has noted that the largest growth of population in America is found among minority groups, and the fastest growth in small businesses is often found among women and minority entrepreneurs. Corporate America cannot afford to ignore this trend, because these are the future purchasers of services and provide many opportunities for strategic partnerships to secure federal and state procurement contracts and employment within the supplier diversity programs within the private sector.

Minority-Owned Businesses as Advocates for Diversity

My business, when hired as a contractor, can help a large corporation communicate that it is an advocate of diversity and employs contractors from traditionally disadvantaged networks as a good corporate actor. Just refer to the US Census Bureau's March 21, 2006 press release that reported the extraordinary growth in Hispanic-owned businesses, "The number of Hispanic-owned businesses grew 31 percent between 1997 and 2002 – three times the national average for all businesses – according to a new report, *Survey of Business Owners: Hispanic-Owned Firms: 2002* [PDF], released today by the U.S. Census Bureau. The nearly 1.6 million Hispanic-owned businesses generated nearly $222 billion in revenue, up 19 percent from 1997."

This change cannot be ignored by the traditional business sector. In 2006, the US Census Bureau also reported that the number of Asian-American businesses grew 24 percent between 1997 and 2002. My state, New Jersey, is ranked third in the number of Asian-American owned businesses. The number of African-American firms grew by 45 percent during the same time period. The number of women-owned businesses grew 20 percent between 1997 and 2002, twice the national average for all businesses, according to a January 2006 U.S. Census Bureau report. "The nearly 6.5 million businesses generated more than $940 billion in revenue, up 15 percent from 1997," according to the press release.

Finding Strength in Diversity

Change is coming, and everyone must be on board. In July 2006, I was named one of the *Courier Post* daily newspaper's first Champions of Diversity for my advocacy on behalf of women- and minority-owed businesses. Active in the Unity Day program for Gloucester County's Human Relations Commission that promotes cross-cultural appreciation and cooperation, I believe that a diverse nation can help make America a stronger nation, if all the groups work together to respect cultural differences. As the below statements will highlight, race, gender, ethnicity, and cultural differences can no longer be ignored by the American mainstream.

Growth of Women-Owned Businesses

Here is a startling fact from the Center for Women's Business Research (*www.womensbusinessresearch.org*): "Businesses majority-owned by women of color have grown six times faster than all U.S. firms between 1997 and 2004. The number of firms increased by more than half (55 percent), number of employees increased by nearly two-thirds (62 percent), and annual sales revenue increased by almost three quarters (74 percent)."

The Center for Women's Business Research also quoted a national business leader on growth trends among women-owned firms. "Women-owned firms are growing and increasing their employment faster than the general market. These firms are driving growth in the American workplace, while generating revenues at a similar rate to all firms. This is a powerful statement about this fast-growing segment of American small business owners," said Joy Ott, Regional President for Wells Fargo in Montana and National Spokesperson for Wells Fargo's Women's Business Services Programs.

It is foolish to ignore these numbers. I volunteer as an ambassador to help build awareness in the corporate sector about these new business trends and the potential impact on business advocacy and leadership.

Raising the Profile of Minority- and Women-Owned Businesses

Like my peers, I attend as many lumber shows, construction networking forums, and meetings with traditional chamber leaders to reinforce our company's outstanding track record in service and to remind them those women in business are indeed successful and can serve as business role models.

Greatest Impact of Innovation in the Workplace

As I think about the greatest impact of innovation in my workplace, I would say that it is a result of comments from my workers in the plant. These men are the front lines, and they handle the wood, process it with equipment, and notice if there are problems with the quality of our products. They are my eyes and ears, and I trust them to bring to my attention any and all problems so we can fix them, prevent loss of income for the company, and succeed in keeping our customers pleased with a superior product.

The Keys to Successful Innovation

What accounts for U.S. Lumber's great success? I credit the company vision built upon teamwork, hard work and strong customer services the foundation for our innovation. My company's motto is, "We're Fast. We're Reliable. We Care." This message says it all. Our full-service minority-certified company has 30 years of wholesale and retail experience. Hard work and keeping abreast of new trends in the construction and lumber industries are the main ingredients for U.S. Lumber's success.

As our industry becomes more mechanized, I still believe we need to rely on talented and dedicated professionals who will be able to subjectively judge quality. A robot can measure the size of something, but can it give insight into the look or feel of wood? I think not. However, I too am concerned about how globalization will affect my workplace organization and employee structure. Every employee receives an employee handbook, because I want them to know what their rights are and what I expect of them as an employee. In my opinion, unless workers know they are respected, they will not perform to their full capabilities. I value my team, and I hope they feel the same way about me.

Volunteering and Giving Back to the Community

However, another part of the innovation toolbox is U.S. Lumber's emphasis on community service. Because I came to America as an immigrant and worked my way up the ladder, I understand the values of kindness and sharing. Certainly, my husband has believed in my management skills and trusted me to grow our company and at the same time be an active advocate of community service and volunteerism. A company can be successful and also have a heart with its employee relations and community advocacy, and that's what we do at U.S. Lumber.

A recipient of the 2003 "Tribute to Women and Industry's Woman of Outstanding Achievement" presented by the YWCA of Camden County, and the Hudson County Asian Business Award, I views my role as a mentor and teacher for others. To continue that tradition, I joined the 2006 Board of Directors of the Girl Scouts of South Jersey Pines. Starting with high school students, I participated in Glassboro High School's Career Day, and highlighted choices available to students in the travel and tourism industry.

An Evaluator for the Hospitality Management Program offered by Gloucester County Institute of Technology, I believe in sharing my knowledge with others to help them work toward the achievement of the American dream. Education is the foundation for all growth, and sharing with the community helps our business remain a great community partner. I never know where the next CEO I will work with might come from, and it would make me very happy to see the Girl Scouts encourage entrepreneurship and business leadership among the many girls served with programming.

Three Greatest Challenges to Cultivating an Innovative Workforce

On the issue of three greatest challenges in cultivating an innovative workforce, it would be remiss not to mention the incredible courage it takes for someone to share an idea. Consequently, an employer must fashion a workplace structure that nurtures and encourages open dialogue and does not "punish" someone for taking a risk to suggest another way of achieving a goal. I admire someone who takes risks. That is the key task for a CEO. We take calculated risks. Therefore, I cultivate an environment where questions are encouraged and rewarded. Of course, I am the boss, and the final decision-making power rests with me. But I can be educated and shown new ways of thinking, especially when we can provide our services more cost effectively.

My three challenges to innovation are:

- Building trust that cultivates
- Assessing the value of innovation first, and cost second
- Pushing for diversity consistently

No change and certainly no innovation will emerge without a trusting relationship between employees and senior management. Companies must have a trusting relationship as the foundation for innovation before any positive changes can be realized.

We recognize the bottom line when assessing profitability and the delivery of services but make a commitment to first understand the nature of innovation and its long-range impact prior to rejecting it because of short-term investment costs. Change takes time and money as do strategic reforms that will promote innovation. Try to be patient with this reality.

No matter what, diversity must be an accepted value in all workplace organizations and has to be embraced by management, owners and shareholders. America in 2006 is not the America of 1955. The business sector must change.

Financial Vision

The life blood of any business is cash flow as it relates to enhancing profitability and growth. Many successful businesses reach a crisis as they grow because of an inability to fashion a pragmatic strategic growth plan that incorporates sensible risk-taking with significant expansion. The key is not to upset customer relations that in turn will affect the bottom line profit rates.

In many ways, the financial vision for the company is based on the personal vision of the CEO. If you believe that the company is an extension of your personal values, you will create a business culture that, in my case, underscores professionalism, respect, and strategic vision based on valuing employee's creative contributions. I am a "hands-on" CEO, meaning that I visit the floor daily and want to hear from the employees about anything that can improve the company. I hear about layers or filters that prevent CEOs from having direct contact with employees or those who have the ideas to improve company operations. What a mistake. Let's share the recognition for great ideas by having ways for the CEO to speak with employees on a regular basis.

Annually, I set a goal of increasing my lumber company's growth by $1 million dollars in annual sales. Of course, when we first began the business, my goals were smaller, but always with the focus of growing larger. Sometimes, when the economy is performing poorly, I may not be able to meet that objective; nonetheless, I still "think big" in order to set a high bar for achievement.

Last year, with sales over $6 million annually, my business experienced key growth again. Being a minority and women-owned and certified business, US Lumber Inc. is successful in marketing itself as filling a unique niche in the lumber and construction related fields. Each time I am honored by my peers nationally, regionally and statewide, my business achieves greater recognition and visibility, and in turn, I believe the long-term benefit comes to my company continuing to grow and be profitable.

If I assessed the breakdown of my year-to-year goals in areas of business performance, I assess them in these percentages.

- Financial Performance – 40%
- New Product Introductions – 50%
- Organizational Goals – 5%
- Other Related Issues – 5%

A CEO sets the tone for an organization. I believe that when you act respectfully, others will respond in kind, that is if they share your value system. Customer relations are so important to our small business that I am responsible for cultivating new customers and working with our existing customer base to serve their needs. Regularly, I call our customers to discuss with the lead staff person, project manager, and budget contact the progress with delivery of services and ways to improve our services. Often, I will offer to attend prospective client meetings with one of my businesses in order to establish a relationship with the prospective project manager and supervisor for the construction and lumber job. They need to see, before I get the job as a contractor, that I have a direct interest in their success. This process has been successful for US Lumber, and it will continue as long as I am owner and CEO.

When it comes to competitors, I am aware of their clients and job growth, but I do not measure US Lumber's success against that of these competitors. Some of my competitors possess businesses that are significantly larger than mine and are not women or minority-owned and certified businesses. One of my goals continues to focus on ways to communicate with large competitors that my business might be an excellent resource to retain for small construction projects that can be met by a woman or minority-owned firm. Many government contracts ask for large companies to include small business contractors within the mix of vendors, and US Lumber is available for that task. With that in mind, I set a 20-25% growth goal annually.

Responsible for business planning as it relates to the establishment of year-to-year goals, I work hard and invest considerable time into helping plan strategic visibility for the business. As the President and CEO, my efforts are the lead ones in elevating the business. Working with the corporate sales manager and director of operations, we set forth objectives. Let me also indicate that being involved in strategic business networks among women and minority-owned and certified businesses has elevated my visibility, resulted in national recognition from my peers in the Asian-American business community, National Association of Women Owned businesses and most recently from the Philippine government as an exceptional role model in America.

With a growth in profit, our managers benefit from incentive plans. This is a flexible program because everything is based on the bottom line. Most of my time is spent securing sales because without sales our company will cease to exist.

Outstanding customer service results in exceptional growth. This strategy has been one implemented from our first day of business operations and I cannot emphasize how strategic our growth has been because of outstanding customer relations.

If our profit is a high percentage, then I know the customer service is working.

Of course, each customer is unique, and therefore, I have mapped out a strategy for each one individually. This takes time, but it affects my bottom line and is well worth the effort.

I would caution newer CEOs to look carefully at poor planning and poor execution of goals, because these two facts can undermine all business operations. Expanding without adequate capital and available cash flow can "kill" business, especially when heavy equipment investments are necessary.

That is why I emphasize great customer relations, starting with my calling each customer, visiting on the road, and doing the cold calls, that are necessary to have business growth.

At the beginning of each New Year, I have a staff meeting with all the staff to mark our previous year's accomplishments and to acknowledge the contributions all our staff has made to the company's success. Throughout the year we may have periodic meetings, but first meeting of the year sets the tone.

Communicating directly with our staff has a profound impact on the employees because they realize their collective impact on company operations and profitability. Company leadership that are distant from their staff's face the challenge of how to motivate employees and, more importantly, how to set-up key networks so senior management learns when there are problems in delivering services. I want to know the good and bad news so I can adjust my leadership role and delivery of customer services in response to challenges. So, lines of communication must be open between the CEO/President, senior managers and the employees.

The prospect of international business is not readily available to my business. However, I am always open to new ideas, and welcome the opportunity to be part of a strategic business team that might engage in bringing entrepreneurship opportunities to other women and minority businesses throughout the globe. Additionally, I welcome the opportunity to meet other successful immigrants to America who opened award-wining businesses and have experienced growth. You never know where business opportunities may surface, and it takes a special drive and determination for someone to leave his or her native land and start out without contacts in a new country. That is my story. And, I was able to turn a horrific experience when I was held against my will by an American employer in my first job in America and had to escape from this building and call immigration because my life was being threatened. Sometimes, adversity reminds us of how strong we are, and how our spirit and faith can sustain us in times where test our being. America has given me an opportunity to share the wealth my company earns with my employees, my family, and through my philanthropic support of community organizations that empower young women and others to achieve greatness. The CEO has the opportunity to inspire or to merely treat employees as objects that make money for the company but have no other value. I have chosen to inspire others and benefit from their desire to provide the best services possible. I encourage my peers to do the same.

CHAPTER FIVE

Women Empowering Women

A female colleague recently asked me, "How many Women's Organizations do you belong to? And where do you find the time to be so interactive with each of them?" I could see it was a surprise to her when I answered, "As many as I can…and I make the time depending on what the other women are like." She had clearly been expecting to hear about some secret formula or a ratio of time vs. effort, but my answer stands. It depends on the women.

You see, if I'm being honest, what makes me join an organization and what makes me choose to stay are two very different things. Not only have my goals changed in recent years, but so have the needs I get from each organization. Choosing one has become less about the trade, industry or potential exposure and more about how we treat each other once we commit to *common* goals.

In my 35 years of entrepreneurship, recognitions and mentoring, the most meaningful part of women who empower other women comes down to how we treat each other as we are working together to achieve said common goals. We may be heading to the same place, but how we walk the path together determines what will bring us success, or otherwise. It has taken me quite some time to come to terms with the idea that just because an organization is comprised of all women, it does not inherently suggest that we are all treated as sisters.

If our collective female voice fails to speak respectfully to and amongst all women, then we remain divided.

Defining All Women, One Voice

I have participated in many groups, associations, and committees that seductively publicize efforts to put forth positive, supporting messages of women empowering women. I have participated in them, I have mentored for some, I have been mentored by others….and I have also *quit*. I say this, not to speak of negativity. Rather to speak of having the choice to seek and find the *right* supporting women who can empower the choices I make for my future. The ones that share my vision, align with my insights and feed my motivations. Women who respect who I am, where I've come from and where I plan on going. Not all female empowerment is created equal.

I recall a time in the not-so-distant past when my participation on an international Board of Directors was a source of great disappointment and setback. I had worked hard to grow my career and my business accolade in order to be invited onto a coveted Board like this; the potential of influence and advancement for my company was right there within reach. Nevertheless, I soon realized that my worth to the organization was defined by my bank account contributions when my first public Board question was, "what is your budget?" Had this female CEO taken the time to discover what other values I could bring to the table, whether by my business experience or my influences in international Higher Education, she would have exhibited supportive leadership rather than the self-serving importance of existing money or power. You see, when women actually empower other women, *together* we realize the money and power that can facilitate change in the world.

It seems I am not the only female businesswoman to have stumbled onto this observation. *Forbes* contributor Lisa Quast has suggested that women are somehow hardwired from childhood to fight with one another for attention and success.[1] Hers, along with other study results, find that this 'anti-woman' pattern can potentially lead to workplace bullying. In fact, *The Wall Street Journal* quotes that "70% of women are bullied by other women."[2]

*"There is a special place in h*** for women who don't help other women."*

— Madeleine Albright —

Given a gender culture where these "Mean Girls" theories may exist, I have become comfortable putting myself first. How? I have stepped down from prestigious appointments, including that of national Board of Director positions. Why? Due to organizational leadership that failed to speak *to* me and *for* me in that unified and magnificent voice we all deserve. Even in all female organizations, we are not united in one voice if our goals and needs do not align. For instance, as mentioned, I have resigned from appointments due to misalignments such as a *primary* focus on making money from members rather than providing a service, or a need for Public Relations to outweigh the resources provided. Self-appointed leaders, selfish administrators, and those who "assign" how I will participate, rather than "invite" my unique skills and knowledge are all Mean Girls I have left behind. None of these concepts were aligned with *my* voice and were therefore not places where I was able to find one voice for all women.

The Change is Upon Us

What does 'Women Empowering Women' look like? As women, we will take responsibility for our own actions toward other women regardless of where they may be in age, career or personal growth. We will;

- Be conscious of the personal ailments, afflictions and pressures we place on one another. They have no place in an empowering community.
- Remember the shoes you've walked in to get to where you are.
- Speak kindly, respectfully and honestly to each woman that crosses your path. They too are walking this journey in the shoes they were given.
- Be humble. There will always be a woman who did it first, did it better or has claimed success for doing it.
- Foster an embracing exchange of differences in culture, origin, status, demographic, etc. A CEO can learn as much from someone else's story as can the student leaving home and heading into college.
- Have a clear plan in place with specific steps for achieving your aspirations in order to keep you focused on your own progress without being worried about what others do, have and want.
- Teach another woman how to create her career development plan.
- Don't judge a book by her cover. We were all sparse details until our stories were written.
- Share your knowledge and don't act like you're the only one who overcame the struggle to learn it the hard way.
- If you have cleared a path, bring someone else along with you. Doing so will not minimize the achievements you yourself have made.

- Make the time. Time is already a commodity; use it wisely to help another woman who has less of it than you do.
- Don't highlight the weaknesses of others with intentions of promoting your own strengths. Success is not a contest – it is a team sport.
- Actively solicit both female and male mentors. The lessons of experience have no gender.
- Have you learned business secrets by working with *men* in male dominated industries? Work on making them Secrets-No-More. In fact, let's stop labeling them "male-dominated-industries" and call them what they are, just "industries".

At the End of the Day…

Ultimately, the concept of women empowering women does not need to come from an organized format of budgeted board meetings and unpaid work after your day job. In fact, you don't need to be a member of something larger to get what you need for your personal or professional growth. If, however, you do choose to surround yourself with the *right* women, that belong to organizational groups or memberships, then do yourself a favor. Do your research, make visiting or volunteering fun, and interview them rather the other way around.

What should you look for in Women's Organizations that have your best interest in mind?

- Those that embrace your members and the value they each bring, not by comparison but by measure of will.
- Those that place a primary goal of furthering the education of its members.
- Those that are drivers of community change by using influence and reach by and amongst its members.

- Those who place importance on the "thank yous" and "pleases", for they will always respect your participation, not just your money.
- Those that offer Mentorship programming that match both mentors and mentees with those having similar goals, but dissimilar backgrounds.

Success doesn't start at the top, it starts at the bottom. To advance beyond the bottom, you must work hard at becoming the leader you wish you had. If you are a leader, you have to be the example you once needed. Sharing goals and expectations with those you choose to align yourself with will ensure that you are not working toward someone else's goal, but instead your own. Consequently, empowering leaders don't just get to the top, they have the opportunity to pull along those who have helped to support them during the journey.

When goals are aligned, empowerment is collective. No woman is left alone when we speak in one magnificently powerful voice for all.

Bibliography/References

1 Women Helping Other Women? Lisa Quast, Forbes Magazine, 2010. *https://www.forbes.com/sites/work-in-progress/2010/11/15/women-helping-other-women-not-so-much-it-seems/#3f7b2a576299*

2 When Women Derail Other Women in the Office, Rachel Emma Silverman, The Wall Street Journal, 2009. *https://blogs.wsj.com/juggle/2009/01/29/when-women-derail-other-women-in-the-office/*

CHAPTER SIX

Going Against the Grain

As an Asian-American leader in what I consider the "second part" of my life, what I am today has been determined by the "first part." My life's challenges began in my hometown of San Pablo City, in Laguna, Philippines. As a young adult and mother, I had become a Catholic school teacher. Even with a degree from a university, I had very few resources and the salary as a teacher was inadequate to meet the needs of several generations of my impoverished family. I HAD to make a better life and a better future for my family.

Fast forward to 2021. I, Isabelita Marcelo Abele, am President and CEO of the family-owned and Southern New Jersey-based U.S. Lumber, Inc. I have successfully gone "against the grain" and positioned my certified woman and minority-owned lumber and building materials company as a regional leader in sales. As a woman in a field dominated by men, I have not let my gender, accent, or my 4-feet, 11-inces height deter me from making my dreams for the company a reality. This chapter is about the major disruptions and adjustments that have marked my transformation from Catholic teacher to a leader in the corporate world. I was able to draw on inner strength, fortitude, risk-taking, and competencies from my cultural heritage as well as from the active pursuit of new skills, knowledge, and expertise.

Dreaming of America

The most exposure I had to a different world was from watching television. Television showed an affluent life in the United States. I can remember that, like many others around me, the soap opera 'Dynasty' captured my imagination. I was intrigued by the female lead, Joan Collins. Were people really living like that? Would it be possible? My Philippine family is very humble, but I dreamed of having more opportunities and a life just like Joan. I dreamed that someday I would open and run my own company. It was then that I set my sights on America and did everything I could to get myself there…no matter what it took.

With relentless tenacity I had applied to every recruiting agency that came into my small town. Again and again my applications were dismissed. The risk of not achieving my goal was high and the strain on my emotional stamina was getting thin. Nevertheless, I did not veer from my path. I kept my focus on my dream.

Unmet Expectations – Dashed Hopes

At last, I finally landed my ticket to the Big Apple in 1981, with nothing but hopes and dreams in my pocket. I was sadly and suddenly disappointed by the circumstances within which I found myself. Upon arrival in America, I took my first job as a maid, cleaning girl, and nanny. I expected to work in a big "homey" house surrounded by wealth, jewels, and food. What I had not expected was to become a mistreated domestic worker and held against my will by that first employer. It took months of planning and praying, but eventually I fled one afternoon, quite literally, while the employer was out. Making a dash to the nearest phone booth with a quarter in my pocket, I sought the assistance of a gracious friend who allowed me to hide in the safety of her home. This initial experience became my next major disruption on the long road to the anticipated 'Joan Collins lifestyle".

Developing Leadership Competencies

The struggle to escape still seems unreal and is seared in my memory even though this was many, many years ago. I reflect upon those days with sadness until I remember that I triumphed in the end. My journey took me through many bends along the road: some o them joyful, some of them laborious; however, none of them stopped me I learned to show gratitude, perseverance, open-mindedness, and respect for tradition that I now use to lead my new life. In fact, from the perspective that I have developed throughout the years, I believe that leadership itself is a collection of learned skills that increases your ability to guide those around you. For me, the most important piece of becoming a true leader has been the ongoing growth of my own open-mindedness and learning to avoid considering challenges as personal, aside from absorbing their lessons. There were days that seemed lie an endless exercise in perseverance and a test of my commitment to my life-long goals of becoming a businesswoman. Other days helped me feel gratitude and appreciation for the role models of my Philippine heritage. What is the bottom line? All lessons are learned and earned but must be applied to move forward.

Working Smarter

The first of those lessons is that starting a new life can be full of hardships. Specifically, emigrating from another country with the intent to build a better life can be a long and lonely journey, no matter where you are coming from. Critical to persevering that dream of a new life is reminding yourself that there will also be endless joy and possibility. What does this mean for those attempting to break through the barriers and avoid being taken off-course? Sometimes it could mean having to work harder and smarter than people who do not have the extra challenge of being from a diverse background. In my case, I never dared to doubt the outcome.

Living and Sharing our Cultural Values

The journey itself has taken me far from the place where I began. I am not talking about San Pablo City: I am talking about the traditions and lessons that our Filipino ancestors taught their children ad then their children's children, and so on. Each of us has a responsibility to continue teaching new generations so that they too can reach for those dreams of learning, growing, and climbing corporate ladders if they choose. An important part of the effort to make change in the lives of those we love is to pass along all the culture and values that many of us grew up with in our homeland. Heritage relies on people like you and me spreading the lessons we were born into so that new generations, whether born her in the USA or back home in another country, can benefit from our rich cultural traditions and legacies.

Showing Respect

Simply put, I learned from my parents and they learned from their parents, and so on. I can remember that as a child, one of our consistent messages was to show respect toward everyone, not just those who are older than you. This was something my parents, grandparents, aunts, and uncles always insisted upon without fail. Children were taught social guidelines at a young age: only speak when spoken to use your "pleases" and "thank you' s" and never EVER interrupt a grown-up; the usual *constructs of good manners. The difference was that these rules were never to be broken, no matter* what! Sometimes all it took was a stern glance from my mothers, and we kids knew not to do whatever "bad thing" we were thinking of doing. That look on her face said everything. You know the one? My kids know it too. But even more importantly, so do my clients.

Valuing Family

I am sure that my fellow Filipino Americans have much in common with the way we grew up. And if I am right, most of us came from homes that also believed that "family" and "respect" were two of the most important building blocks in the foundation of our culture. As a Filipino-American female entrepreneur, it is this core of Filipino values that I recognize have helped me achieve what I have achieved. In fact, after years and years of learning from different people and different sources, I have come to value what my culture has provided me. The family values have stayed with me in my voyage from a struggling teacher in my hometown of San Pablo City to a mistreated main in New York City to the executive role as President of a multi-million-dollar U.S. corporation.

Using Family Values To Grow My Business

As the baby of four children in my family, I am the only one who has made my way to the United States and a career in the business world. Of my three siblings, my older brother and I were always more similar to each other than the others were. Family values were instilled into all our lives, but somehow my older brother and I had a special connection. In fact, when we lost him several years ago, I tried helping as many of his 10 children as I could at that time. While I was certainly no Joan Collins, I was fortunate to be in a better position to help financially. Coming from a background and culture that places importance on close relationships has taught me this is the most valuable thing we can learn and teach each other. The kinship and security that a big family can give you means very little in the business world without truly embracing the lessons about helping one another, supporting relatives and community, and showing respect to all people, young or old, family or otherwise.

Being Strong and Persistent

I truly believe that my culture and heritage gave me the strength and persistence to move away from distraction, to embrace the struggle, and to go against the grain when necessary. I use many of those foundational social constructs that we learned long ago to directly help build good client relationships. Truth, honesty, colleagues, and customers. A consistent practice of telling employees, vendors, and clients exactly what the company needs from them, or what I expect from them, creates a fair and genuine starting point for lasting relationships. On the flip side, I make it a practice to listen to employees, clients, and other industry stakeholders I believe that it has been my family history that provided the good habits of setting expectations and creating strong two-way lines of communication where questions are always welcomed and are considered important. As a result, building trust is a vital piece of maintaining my good reputation with customers and business connections. We proclaim this loudly as our company slogan, "We're fast. We're reliable. We care."

Building Relationships

Building good relationships with my clients has not always been easy. I struggled for many years, and sometimes still do, with the challenge of speaking English as a second language. I felt disrespected by some clients and vendors who thought they had the right to make negative comments. "Here comes the tiny woman in the hard hat that can't pronounce her words." Sometimes they were even rude enough to pretend to understand what I said and made me repeat it, over and over again.

I may never lose the accent with which I learned to speak English, but there was never a reason not to READ, READ, READ. I would read anything I could get my hands on and let myself be immersed with new ideas, thoughts, and information. The more I learned and became fluent in specialized vocabulary I needed to run my company, the more confident I became with my knowledge. Perseverance was the key. The rude clients and vendors did not get to me. They only made themselves appear to be less professional and more like bullies. My integrity, resolve, and manners are always intact. Remember, the voice that speaks to you in your own head does not have to speak perfect English, and neither does the one that speaks to everyone else.

Turning a Negative into a Positive

At times, it would have been easier to just run away when I experienced challenges. It was important to remind myself that if I allowed someone to get me off course, I would be handing them my hard-earned power and respect. Each day required that I be stronger than the day before, look adversity in the face, and remind myself that 'ignorance has no first language.' I refused to allow these experiences to make a negative person of me. Eventually, my accent became my calling-card to some very unique relationships. My voice can never be mistaken for someone else's. After many years, my accent is still the best part of me; my friends and clients never question who is calling on the phone! Consequently, this also differentiates me as well as my business proposals from others and I do not hesitate to point this out. I remain proud of my differences and teach others about me and my culture whenever I have the chance. This sharing of backgrounds only makes everyone stronger and smarter, along with the relationship itself. The people in my life may never forget who I am because of the accent; it is up to me to give them a favorable impression of the rest of me. Open-mindedness was the key to turning relationships around, language barriers or not.

Being Different is a Positive

One of the greatest gifts I learned to share with the different people in my life is that it is okay to be different. I have always held that being different truly means that each of us has a variety of experiences and knowledge that no other individual has. Whether it's a prominent accent or a family with rich heritage, being different provides the opportunity to use your unique perspective to drive a new life.

When I came to America, I promised myself that I would never hide my talent and abilities. In fact, not hiding my abilities is central to my personal philosophy as I am now also better able to celebrate and nurture the talents of others.

Improving One's Self

Ever since I gave birth to my BIG dreams based on what I had seen on television, I have always tried to remember who I was. No matter how difficult the struggle, I never lost sight of the idea that something better lies ahead. What helped me to focus on the end goal was the belief that we should do more than just work on our businesses but strive to work on ourselves. International organizations like the Filipina Women's Network, along with my local Asian-American Chamber of Commerce and the National Association of Professional Asian American women, have been important resources for me. Not only are they able to offer professional materials for an entrepreneur, but they also provide support, role modeling, and inspiration from some of the great women who have come before us.

Being Role Models

Another aspect of our business is helping our community by being role models. This belief in being role models has been the driving force behind much of my participation in business, local and national association boards, fundraisers, and projects along the way. Of the many core lessons, I have learned from my ancestors and the Filipino culture, is that helping people in all facets of their lives is what creates a strong and diverse community. It is our responsibility to pass these lessons along to the next generations.

I am certain that this is how my parents and grandparents felt when they taught us to embrace" the spirit of being hospitable to guests." It is part of the Filipino culture to be open and ready at all times, to share your heart and your home while making people feel welcome. This means everyone, whether they are family, friends, neighbors, out of town guests, or even business associates. It is because of this belief in opening myself to community that I put so much of my own effort into fundraising and volunteer activities. My family is often right by my side since I volunteer their time as well as my own.

Because my family respects me and my leadership actions, they happily participate and engage with the community.

Building Community

My husband Merrill and I have hosted many business events in our home. We go beyond the annual holiday party where each of our employees, their spouses, and even the children, are welcome at a family style feast and celebration. We extend invitations to events to the wider community throughout the year. The intent is to establish partnerships, craft new agreements, and to allow for mutli-national endeavors to drive toward new collective goals while paving the way for our youth to learn from others. My family and I call this 'supporting community from a personal perspective.'

Going Beyond

By multi-national endeavors I mean that we must think BIG. After all, it was a big dream that brought me to where I am, and only big, shared, dreams will take me to new heights. My family and I have hosted at our home, for example, the staff of the Philippine Consulate General of New York in order to work on the relationship between Rowan University, a large New Jersey state college, and the University of the Philippines College of Engineering. By working closely with the

University Board of Trustees and academic leaders, we are supporting collaboration between the universities that will improve both. We have also hosted at our home receptions for the Girl Scouts of America to support their mission of 'helping build girls of courage, confidence and character, who make the world a better place.'

Accepting Help

We know we cannot do it all alone. Having the perseverance and drive to achieve your goals while staying on course are often only one piece of the recipe. Learning to accept assistance from those around you who are willing to contribute to your success is a critical lesson.

For the contemporary female entrepreneur, businesswoman, and mother, learning to ask for help is not always easy. There is no shame in asking for assistance, but no one can help if you remain silent about your needs. Most people do seek ways to help others because it makes them feel good. Take advantage of opportunities to join forces and create partnerships.

CHAPTER SEVEN

Personal Lessons for Women & Minorities from Lita Abele

The following questions were posed to Lita Abele who shares her candid and authentic views with the female aspiring or current leader:

What Have Been Lessons Learned From The Pandemic Of 2020?

1. Focus on your needs rather than your wants.
2. Learn to simplify.
3. Embrace the importance of family.
4. Make peace with your past. Stop looking in the rearview mirror.
5. Adjust and find new 'normal' during crisis.
6. Pray for all people of the world and for scientists who created the vaccinations for COVID19
7. To never take a 'normal' life (i.e. pre-pandemic) for granted again.

What Has Been Your Greatest Success?

Without a doubt, being CEO of US Lumber, Inc.

What Was Greatest Obstacle On Your Journey?

My first employer when arriving to the USA from the Philippines as I was abused and disrespected,

What Is Your Advice For Minority Women Entering The Workplace?

1 Work hard and be determined.
2 Bring your culture with you.
3 Use common sense.
4 Be persistent.
5 Love and enjoy what you do.

What Can Companies Do To Provide Equality?

1 Treat all employees as equals.
2 Put themselves into the employee's "shoes" regarding personal issues or stress-related work problems.
3 Have empathy.
4 Create an open-door policy for productive communication.

What Can Women Do When Faced With Discrimination And Be Stronger In The Workplace?

1 See stereotyping as a challenge to be overcome. Prove the stereotype wrong (i.e. gender, race, nationality). Show them what you have to offer and your strengths.

2 Don't take the bait!

3 Don't second-guess your own worth.

4 Be calm and not over-reactive.

5 Be true to your values and integrity

6 Don't gossip.

7 If you have an accent, embrace it.

8 Be approachable and confident

9 Use personal charm. Don't let them see you sweat!

How Did You Gain The Courage To Run Your Own Company?

1 I have always been a dreamer.

2 I reflected back upon the changes and transformation from my life of poverty until now.

3 I have never looked down upon family members living in poverty but embrace my connection to them.

4 I am committed to sharing with others and helping with college scholarships

5 I share my knowledge with other women.

6 I embrace my talents and gifts. This gives me courage to overcome any challenges past or present.

What Challenges Have You Faced From Clients And With You Being Female And Asian, How Did You Deal With Them?

1 I was treated very poorly in the beginning when I started out in our business at entry level.

2 We lost a client who would not deal with an Asian.

3 Because of my accent, clients would ask "Who are you?"

4 I showed the biased clients this Asian woman was not a dummy!

5 Regardless of treatment, I acted respectfully but assertively.

6 Now as CEO, because I treat others within the company and clients with respect, I am also respected. I feel I have earned their respect.

7 I am committed to building relationships.

8 Even if a client chooses to move on, I will not be manipulated nor walked on. However, I will not be rude.

How Do You Overcome Fear?

1 Prayer: I ask for guidance, strength, calmness, and peace

2 Remind myself "I can do it!"

3 Be honest with myself about the fear. Embrace the feeling but strategize how to overcome the fear.

How Did You Change During The Pandemic?

1 I learned not to complain and accept what was.

2 Adapted to running the business from home, which at first was very stressful.

3 Changed my diet and adapted to eating well on a more restrictive diet with healthy foods.

4 Understand my basic needs to survive while living in isolation during pandemic.

5 I realized the importance of adjustment.

6 Learned to tighten the belt financially.

7 I didn't know about tomorrow so embraced today.

8 I had time for self-reflection.

9 I became more thankful for everything and everyone in my life.

What Are Basic Leadership Skills You Have Used And Suggest For Women?

1 Be strong.

2 Be focused. Apply your knowledge and experience.

3 Be persistent.

4 Fine-tune your listening skills. Most leaders are stereotyped as excellent speakers, but the best leaders are also gifted listeners.

5 Deep sense what others are feeling.

6 Have empathy.

7 Be an encourager.

8 Communicate with others always. Don't shut people out.

9 Be a creative problem-solver. Think outside the box.

10 Be pro-active note reactive.

11 Look at the BIG picture and learn to prioritize your tasks to accomplish your goals.

Who Are People You Admire?

1 All those hard working individuals who became successul but remained humble, respectful, and down to earth.

2 My second employer: smart, loving, considerate, gave compliments, helped with education, encouraged, honest, and treated me like family.

3 Neighbor after arrival in NY – safety, a place to live, encouraged, and was treated like family.

4 My son and daughter for staying strong when I left.

5 Linda Ellis Eastman: I dreamed about publishing a book and she inspired me to write. She is my publisher.

6 Mr. Henry Rowan, a very successful businessman who donated 100 million dollars to Rowan University (formerly Glassboro State College) to enhance the education provided to students, especially the Engineering Department. Rowan University became the 2nd in the Nation with two Medical School & Research Institutes.

7 Linda Rohrer: Trustee of William Rohrer foundation, founded by her father, has donated to Rowan University, hospitals, and other universities. The William Rohrer Business School at Rowan University was named after her father.

8 My parents for helping me on my life journey.

What Was Your Greatest Challenge Transitioning From The Philippines To Life In The Usa?

1 Language and expressions.

2 Culture

3 Feeling alone.

4 Being away from family.

5 Difficulty being judged by my appearance and accent.

If You Could Do It All Over Again, What Would You Change?

1 I would not leave my children. A gap was created.

CHAPTER EIGHT

Awards & Accolades & Photographs

2022

- Philadelphia Titan 100 Top CEO & Level Executives

2021

- HSB Top Women in Hardware & Building Supply

2019

- St. Magdalene of Canossa Alumni for Professional /Leadership Award
- USPAACC-Top 10 Regional Asian American Business Award
- PWN International Advisory Board member

2018

- Top 100 Women in Business Philadelphia Business Journal

2017

- Women of Excellence Inspiration Award: SJ Magazine
- Woman Business Owner of the Year – NAWBO
- 100 Most Influential Filipina Women in the World – Filipina Women's Network
- Top 25 Minority Own #7 Philadelphia Business Journal
- 2017 FASSJ Love Award by Filipino American Society of Southern NJ

2016

- USPAACC Top 100 Asian American Business Excellence Award
- Brava Awards Honouring Top Female CEO by Smart CEO's Philadelphia

2015

- The Alice Paul Institute's Equality Award
- Top South Jersey Entrepreneurs by Philadelphia Business Journal

2014

- Superwomen of the Year award by South Jersey Magazine
- Women of Achievement Award from the Gloucester Commission on Women
- Smart CEO Circle of Excellence Award

2013

- Outstanding Entrepreneurs by South Jersey Biz Magazine
- Top 50 Minority Owned Company by Philadelphia Business Journal

- Finalist for Circle of Excellent by Smart/CEO
- Outstanding Asian American Business Award by Asian American Chamber of Commerce Of Greater Philadelphia
- Top 100 Women in Business by Philadelphia Business Journal

2012

- Dr. Jose P. Rizal Circle Excellence Award in Business.
- Centennial Award in Business By Filipino American Associations of Philadelphia, Inc.

2010

- Stevie Awards Finalist – Best Entrepreneur

2009

- 100 Most Influential Filipina Women in the United States by Filipina Women Network.

2008

- The International Alliance for Women's (TIAW) World of Difference 100
- NJBIZ 50 Best Women in Business

2007

- Selected as one of the 10 Best Outstanding Women in Business by South Jersey Magazine.
- National Stevie Award finalist for the recognition of an Outstanding Achievement in Business and Best Entrepreneur

2006

- Dangalng Lahi Award (Pride of the Heritage Award), Filipino American Centennial Gala
- Awarded Champion of diversity, Courier Post of South Jersey
- Certificate of Recognition for Outstanding Enterprising Women in Business by; Office of the Mayor, City of San Pablo, Philippines

2005

- Top National Finalist, Stevie Award for Women Entrepreneurs
- Gold Star Winner, NAWBO South Jersey
- Top Ten Finalist, Mirassou Optimist Award, NAWBO
- Outstanding 50 Asian Americans in Business Award
- Asian Entrepreneur for Construction by Asian Enterprise Magazine
- Enterprising Woman of the Year, Enterprising Women Magazine, Business Sales – $5 million – $10 million in 2004
- 25 Women of Influence, NJBIZ Magazine
- Outstanding Filipino American In Business by Filipino Heritage Foundation Inc.
- Woman of the Year Award by The Girl Scout of South Jersey Pines

2004

- 25 Women of Influence, Philadelphia Business Journal
- NAWBO South Jersey, Businesswoman of the Year
- Top Ten Finalist, Wells Fargo Asian American Award

2003

- Twin Award Tribute to Women and Industry by YWCA

2002

- AAHC Asian American Achievement Award for Professional & Academic by The Asian American Heritage Council of New Jersey

Board of Trustee Members, Board of Directors, and Advisory Board

Past and Present:

- Rowan University Board of Trustee
- Rowan College Board of Trustee – Secretary
- Rowan University South Jersey Tech Park
- Rowan College Foundation Board
- New Jersey Development Authority for Small Business, Women's & Minorities
- Girl Scout of South Jersey Pines – Board of Directors
- Girl Scout of Central & Southern New Jersey – Board of Directors Secretary
- NJ Asian American Chambers of Commerce – Founding Bd. Member
- Philippine American Chamber of Commerce of NJ-PA – Treasurer – Founding Member
- Filipina Women's Network- Board Member
- Philippine Folk Art Society- Board Member
- Enterprising Women's Magazines- Advisory Board
- Liberty Bank – Advisory Board

Speaking Engagements

- Keynote Speaker Gold Award Celebration:
- Girl Scout of Jersey Pines- Topic "Inspirational

- Guest Speaker: City of Seven Lakes San Pablo City Gala:
- Topic: Success
- Guest Speaker: Deptford Rotary – Deptford New Jersey- Culture & Custome
- Speaker: Filipino Intercollegiate Networking Dialogue (FIND) Culture, Values & Success
- Speaker: Stockton University = Launching of (PASSAS) Filipino American Students Association of Stockton
- Speaker: RUPAC – Rowan University Philippine American Coalition
- Being a supporter/Benefactor

Panelist

- Filipina Women Network: How to Become Filipina Millionaire – Panelist
- Philadelphia Business Journal: Executive Panel 2013 South Jersey Entrepreneurs awards- Inspiring Panel
- Chamber of Commerce Southern New Jersey Women's Conference:
- Journey to C-Suite
- Hardware & Building Supply Dealer: Pursuing Power
- Alliance of Women Entrepreneurs: conference Women's & Minoroties
- Session (SBA)

Enterpreneur of the Year By Enterpreneur Magazine

With Governor Christy Whitman

With Governor James McGrevey

With Governor Ed Rendell and Brittny Petrella

With Senate President Steve Sweeney & Governor Corzine

With NJ Senator Fred Madden

My Parents

My Son and My Daughter
Romilett and Ryan

With My Son's Family

With My Daughter's Family

My Family in Houlton Maine 2nd to Employer

My Extended Filipino Family Who Helped in NYC

25 Women of Influence PBJ with Anchor Tracy Davidson

Enterprising Woman of the Year in Enterprising Women Magazine

100 Most Influential Filipina Women In United States 2009
with Husband Merrill, Daughter and Niece

2017 Most Influential Filipina Woman Globally

Alice Paul Equality Award with Mary Soyka
and Linda Coppinger Board Chair

2005 Outstanding 50 Asian American Business Award

Outstanding Asian American Business Award with Deputy Consul General Zaldy Patron

Dangalang Lahi Award Filipino Centennial Gala w Consul General NY Cecil Rebong

Circle of Excellence Award Smart CEO Magazine

NAWBO Woman Business Owner of the Year
With Marianne Aleardi crop

Philadelphia Titan 100 2022 with
Dr. Ali Houshmand Rowan President

SJ Magazine Women of Excellence and Inspiration Award

PBJ Entrepreneur of the Year Award

Lita with Driver and Yard Employees

Visiting one of the Jobsites

Keynote Speaker and Board Member
for the Girl Scout Gold Award

Networking with Miss World

Brava Award Honoring Female CEO By Smart CEO Magazine

HBS Top Women Hardware & Building Supply

Lita as a Board of Trustee at Rowan University

Panelist How to Become a Filipina Millionaire

Baby sitting Joe and Alice

High School Friends

Our Family

About the Author

As President and CEO of the South Jersey-based, family-owned lumber supplier U.S. Lumber, Inc. Isabelita (Lita) Abele has successfully "gone against the grain" and positioned her certified woman and minority-owned lumber and building materials company as a regional leader in industry sales.

She represents the best of success in American Diversity as she breaks the barriers of the glass ceiling and opens opportunities for Filipino and minority women in America. Her outstanding leadership in a non-traditional woman-owned corporation has been recognized for over twenty-five years with outstanding international, regional, and local business awards and recognition.

Lita spreads her enthusiasm for women empowering women on a regular basis through her participation and membership in women's organizations across the globe, including those that benefit young women. Her motivation to help community extends to her grassroots in teaching and education, where she develops international exchange programs and scholarships for youth entering higher education.

Lita Abele serves on the PWN International Board of Advisors, a organization dedicated to the increased self-esteem and confidence of women globally. She has also coauthored several anthologies providing diversity strategies and lessons for CEO's. Lita is listed on the PWN Author's Bureau at *www.pwnbooks.com*.

PART II
WORKSHEETS

WORKSHEET #1

ACCOMPLISHMENT

What do you consider your greatest accomplishment in life? Provide details and how you achieved this accomplishment:

ACCOMPLISHMENT

Steps to achieving accomplishment:

1 ______________________________

2 ______________________________

3 ______________________________

4 ______________________________

5 ______________________________

6 ______________________________

7 ______________________________

8 ______________________________

9 ______________________________

10 ______________________________

WORKSHEET #2

CHILDHOOD CHALLENGES

What do you consider to be your childhood challenges before the age of sixteen? How did they make you feel?

CHALLENGES

1 ______________________________

2 ______________________________

3 ______________________________

4 ______________________________

5 ______________________________

6 ______________________________

7 ______________________________

8 ______________________________

9 ______________________________

10 ______________________________

What was your #1 childhood challenge? How did you cope or deal with it? Share below.

____

____

____

WORKSHEET #3

CHILDHOOD STRENGTHS/GIFTS

What were your strengths and abilities before the age of sixteen? List below and provide examples.

CHILDHOOD STRENGTHS/GIFTS

1 ______________________________

2 ______________________________

3 ______________________________

4 ______________________________

5 ______________________________

6 ______________________________

7 ______________________________

8 ______________________________

9 ______________________________

10 ______________________________

Greatest success before the age of sixteen:

____

____

____

WORKSHEET #4
CHILDHOOD DREAMS

As a child before the age of sixteen, what was your childhood dream of what you wanted to become as an adult? If you could coach that little girl, what would have been the steps to make that dream come true? Provide the steps below.

CHILDHOOD DREAM

What was the dream? ______________________________

Steps to make your dream come true:

1 ______________________________

2 ______________________________

3 ______________________________

4 ______________________________

5 ______________________________

6 ______________________________

7 ______________________________

8 ______________________________

9 ______________________________

10 ______________________________

Are you living your childhood dream? If not, why? What obstacles got in the way?

____

____

____

WORKSHEET #5

STARTING YOUR CAREER

Reflect back to when you started your career. What obstacles and challenges were you faced with? (i.e. racism, genderism, accent, etc). How did you overcome those challenges?

CAREER CHALLENGES

What was your major challenge in starting a career? ______________

____

List all challenges when you entered your career:

1 ____

2 ____

3 ____

4 ____

5 ____

6 ____

7 ____

8 ____

9 ____

10 ____

WORKSHEET #6

BULLYING

As an adult, at home or at work, have you ever been bullied? Who bullied you, how did you react? What could you have done differently?

BULLYING

Who bullied you and how did you react? (Proactively being assertive and challenging the bullying behavior or Reactive by being overly emotional with crying in front of bully or saying nothing?)

List bully and how you handled the situation:

1 ____________________

2 ____________________

3 ____________________

4 ____________________

5 ____________________

6 ____________________

7 ____________________

8 ____________________

9 ____________________

10 ____________________

Could you have been more assertive in dealing with the bully?

____

WORKSHEET #7

ASSERTIVENESS

Would you consider yourself to be passive (non-confrontational), assertive (stand up for yourself and your views), or aggressive (highly confrontational – your way or no way)?

ASSERTIVENESS

Consider with whom you are passive, those with whom you are open and confident, and those with whom you are aggressive and often angry.

List the people in your personal and proessional lives and note the type of communication behavior you exhibit with each:

1 ______________________________

2 ______________________________

3 ______________________________

4 ______________________________

5 ______________________________

6 ______________________________

7 ______________________________

8 ______________________________

9 ______________________________

10 ______________________________

The healthiest behavior is to be ASSERTIVE. An assertive woman stands up for herself, in spite of opposition, and tactfully expresses her thoughts and feelings while respecting the thoughts and view of others.

With whom can you become more assertive: ____________

WORKSHEET #8

TOXIC RELATIONSHIPS

After the age of sixteen until now, have you ever been in a toxic relationship in your personal life where someone either verbally, physically or emotionally abused you? How about in your professional life where a manager, co-worker or the work environment made you feels poorly about yourself?

TOXIC RELATIONSHIPS

Consider the people in your personal and professional lives who were toxic and made you feel poorly about yourself. What did they do? Did you separate yourself from them? Are you currently in a toxic relationship or work environment?

1 ____

2 ____

3 ____

4 ____

5 ____

6 ____

7 ____

8 ____

9 ____

10 _______________________________________

Toxic relationships in your personal life may involve abuse but also someone who diminished your self-worth and self-value. At work, it may be someone who attempts to undermine your good work or is constantly critical of you.

If you are in a toxic relationship now, with who? ________________

WORKSHEET #9

YOUR STRENGTHS & GIFTS

We all have inherent strengths and gifts. Please reflect below your strengths and how you use those strengths for meeting your own personal needs and helping others.

STRENGTHS	HOW YOU USE THEM
1 ______	
2 ______	
3 ______	
4 ______	
5 ______	
6 ______	
7 ______	
8 ______	
9 ______	
10 ______	

What is your greatest strength? ______

Close your eyes and reflect upon the ways you use your greatest strength for the benefit of the good. What is the most powerful benefit to others? To yourself?

______

______

______

WORKSHEET #10

VALUES

More than anything in life, we all have top values such as family, honesty, fairness, friendship, financial success, etc. But the question is, are you living your authentic life based upon what you value? Do you spend your time and money on what's important to you or are these values moved down your priority list in life as you lack the time to focus on them?

VALUES

What are your topic values in life? List how you're living those values (i.e family – spending each Sunday as family time with sharing of challenges and joys or perhaps you value animal rescue, and you spend time weekly taking shelter dogs for a walk)

1 ______________________________

2 ______________________________

3 ______________________________

4 ______________________________

5 ______________________________

6 ______________________________

7 ______________________________

8 ______________________________

9 ______________________________

10 ______________________________

List your TOP THREE VALUES and how you live them.

1 ______________________________

2 ______________________________

3 ______________________________

WORKSHEET #11

GOALS-LIFETIME

Consider what you want to accomplish in your lifetime. It is best to list all the realistic goals you can complete in your many years on earth. What are your ten top lifetime goals?

TEN TOP LIFETIME GOALS

1 ______________________________

2 ______________________________

3 ______________________________

4 ______________________________

5 ______________________________

6 ______________________________

7 ______________________________

8 ______________________________

9 ______________________________

10 ______________________________

#1 Lifetime Goal: ______________________________

How will you accomplish this goal?

____

____

____

WORKSHEET #12

5-YEAR GOALS

To reach your lifetime goals, it is best to breakdown your strategies into realistic five-year goals and by noting timelines for accomplishing these goals. Take a deep breath and close your eyes. Reflect upon where you are now and where you want to be in five years, both personally and professionally. Consider a date for completion of specific goal.

GOAL **DATE FOR COMPLETION**

1 ______________________________

2 ______________________________

3 ______________________________

4 ______________________________

5 ______________________________

6 ______________________________

7 ______________________________

8 ______________________________

9 ______________________________

10 ______________________________

Most Important 5-Year Goal: ______________________________

What is your strategy for accomplishing this goal?

____

____

____

WORKSHEET #13

1-YEAR GOAL

Now it's time to think deeply about your life as it is now. Are you having any personal challenges with relationships? Your health? Finances? Or professional challenges which make you feel stressed, unfulfilled, or angry? When you look into the mirror, do you love the person in your reflection? Why or why not? Is it time to re-design your life so you are deeply pleased with who you are and what you are doing with your life? Take time now to consider 1-year goals which can serve as a roadmap to where you want to be in the near future, both personally and professionally.

1-YEAR GOAL PERSONAL/PROFSSIONAL

1 ______________________________

2 ______________________________

3 ______________________________

4 ______________________________

5 ______________________________

6 ______________________________

7 ______________________________

8 ______________________________

9 ______________________________

10 ______________________________

#1 One-Year Goal: ______________________________

What is your strategy for accomplishing this goal?

____

____

____

Printed in the USA
CPSIA information can be obtained
at www.ICGtesting.com
JSHW072037220224
57846JS00016B/166